CW00521508

G.

CENGAGE Learning

Novels for Students, Volume 30

Project Editor: Sara Constantakis Rights Acquisition and Management: Leitha Etheridge-Sims, Sari Gordon, Aja Perales, Jhanay Williams Composition: Evi Abou-El-Seoud Manufacturing: Drew Kalasky

Imaging: John Watkins

Product Design: Pamela A. E. Galbreath, Jennifer Wahi Content Conversion: Katrina Coach Product Manager: Meggin Condino © 2010 Gale, Cengage Learning

For product information and technology assistance, contact us at **Gale Customer Support, 1-800-877-4253.**

For permission to use material from this text or product, submit all requests online at **www.cengage.com/permissions.**

Further permissions questions can be emailed to **permissionrequest@cengage.com** While every effort has been made to ensure the reliability of the information presented in this publication, Gale, a part of Cengage Learning, does not guarantee the accuracy of the data contained herein. Gale accepts no payment for listing; and inclusion in the publication of any organization, agency, institution, publication, service, or individual does not imply endorsement of the editors or publisher. Errors brought to the attention of the publisher and verified to the satisfaction of the publisher will be corrected in future editions.

Gale
27500 Drake Rd.
Farmington Hills, MI, 48331-3535

ISBN-13: 978-0-7876-8687-1
ISBN-10: 0-7876-8687-5
ISSN 1094-3552

This title is also available as an e-book.
ISBN-13: 978-1-4144-4946-3
ISBN-10: 1-4144-4946-1
Contact your Gale, a part of Cengage Learning sales
representative for ordering information.

Printed in the United States of America
1 2 3 4 5 6 7 13 12 11 10 09

How Green Was My Valley

Richard Llewellyn

1939

Introduction

How Green Was My Valley is Richard Llewellyn's best-known work, a bestselling novel that was first published in 1939 and was made into a popular movie in 1941. It tells the story of Huw Morgan, the son and brother of coal miners in south Wales at the end of the nineteenth and the beginning of the twentieth centuries, focusing on the destruction of his green valley by the spread of coal mining and the slag heap (a pile of waste material that is a by-product of mining).

Told as a reminiscence of happier times, the novel has a sad, sentimental tone, describing the passing away of many people in Huw's life as well as the loss of his valley's greenness. It is in part a coming-of-age tale, including a sensitive portrayal of Huw's romantic initiation. There is also some description of violence and use of mild profanity.

Although Welsh commentators have criticized the novel for inaccuracies in its portrayal of Wales, it has come to be seen as a portrayal of the essence of Welshness, but the true source of its appeal may have less to do with its specific Welsh setting than with its universal themes of loss and nostalgia.

Author Biography

Richard Llewellyn was the pen name of Richard Herbert Vivian Lloyd. He also went by the name Richard Dafydd Vivian Llewellyn Lloyd. Llewellyn claimed to have been born in Wales, but although he was of Welsh descent, he was actually born in a suburb of London, England, on December 8, 1906. His father worked in hotel management, and Llewellyn at first followed him into that business but left to join the army in 1926, serving in India and Hong Kong. When he returned to London after six years of service, he found work as a reporter for a movie magazine and then began working in the film industry.

According to some reports, Llewellyn had been working on the manuscript of *How Green Was My Valley*, at first called *Slag*, while in India. In London, he wrote a successful play titled *Poison Pen*, from which he found encouragement to work full time on his novel. He completed the manuscript after moving to Llangollen, Wales, and published it in London in 1939, where it was an immediate success. It sold 50,000 copies in England in its first four months of publication, and in America it reached the top of the bestseller list in 1940. It won rave reviews in many locations around the world except in Wales itself, where it was criticized as not being a realistic portrayal of the coal miners. The movie based on it won five Academy Awards including best picture in 1942, and the book was translated into thirteen languages but not Welsh.

Some sources say Llewellyn based the unnamed village in the book on the south Wales mining village of Gilfach Goch. Llewellyn claimed to have worked as a coal miner in the area for research purposes, but it is not clear that this claim is true.

Llewellyn went on to write more than twenty other novels, including three sequels to *How Green Was My Valley*. None of these works matched the success of the original, though Llewellyn did win praise for *None But the Lonely Heart*, his 1943 novel about life among London criminals in the 1930s.

Published in 1960, *Up, into the Singing Mountains* (the first sequel to *How Green Was My Valley*) depicts what happens to Huw after his departure from his Welsh mining village: Huw travels to the Welsh colony in Patagonia in Argentina. In 1966 Llewellyn continued the story of Huw in Patagonia in *Down Where the Moon Is Small*. In the final sequel to *How Green Was My Valley*, *Green, Green My Valley Now* (1975), Huw returns to Wales, where he becomes involved in various movements to revive past Welsh glories.

Details of Llewellyn's life after the publication of *How Green Was My Valley* are scant, but it is known that he was in the Welsh Guards during World War II, though mostly as a noncombatant, and that he traveled widely after the war, in part to research his fiction. In addition to Patagonia, he set his later novels in such places as Israel, India, Kenya, and Brazil.

Llewellyn married Nona Theresa Sonsteby in 1952; the two divorced in 1968. In 1974 he married Susan Frances Heimann and moved with her to Dublin, Ireland, where he died on November 30, 1983.

Chapter 1

How Green Was My Valley begins with the narrator, Huw Morgan, packing up and leaving his valley after having lived his whole life there. As he does this, he begins telling the story of his life, and the rest of the novel consists of this story, presented as he prepares to leave.

He begins with rough but prosperous days when his father and older brothers would come back from the coal mines, laughing and singing and tossing their pay in gold sovereigns (coins) to his mother. He also recounts extravagant Saturday dinners with ham, beef, lamb, and chicken, and the good-natured joking between his father and his mother. However, Huw hints at darker times to come, noting that his father warned him he would come to a bad end and saying that it turns out he was right.

The chapter ends with the first plot development, the meeting between Huw's oldest brother, Ivor, and the girl he is to marry, Bronwen. Huw says he fell in love with Bronwen too even though he was only a child. He ends the chapter on a characteristically sad and nostalgic note by stating all these events have passed.

Chapter 2

This chapter begins with Huw's recollection of the happy wedding of Ivor and Bronwen and includes a characteristic comment by Huw on the strange ways of memory. Huw also recounts the story of the marriage of his second brother, Ianto. Ianto marries a girl of whom his family does not exactly approve, then moves away and is not seen for years. The chapter also introduces a major plot element, the struggle for better wages at the mine, led by yet another of Huw's brothers, Davy, which results in two strikes.

Chapter 3

Huw remembers his first schoolteacher, Mrs. Tom Jenkins, and her badly injured miner husband. Mrs. Jenkins was unhappy enough about her life to question the existence of God, and Huw states that his teacher's thoughts made him think about his own life, which perhaps hurt him over the years. The chapter ends with Huw's recollections of family disagreements over whether to support a big union and Socialism.

Chapter 4

At six years old, Huw feels left out of his family's experiences. He sneaks out of the house at night to attend a union meeting, then falls in a barrel of water trying to get back into the house. His father is waiting for him but only mildly reprimands him.

Chapter 5

Their father'smoderation in union matters annoys Davy and two of Huw's other brothers, Owen and Gwilym. They leave home, which prompts Huw's mother to cry. Observing his mother crying is a disillusioning moment for Huw, because it makes her seem weak and comic to him.

This chapter includes a discussion about the destructive effect of the slag produced by mining: it is causing the valley to turn black. The chapter ends with Huw's father fetching his sons home from their boarding house because of the bad conditions there. Their mother is happy, but Huw's father feels his authority has been compromised.

Chapter 6

The union argument leads to disaster in chapter 6. Huw's mother addresses an outdoor union meeting on a wintry night, telling the men not to threaten her husband or her son Ivor, both of whom are now against the union. She succeeds in intimidating the union men, but on the way home she falls down in the snow. Huw, who is accompanying her, is barely able to save her life— he falls into the icy river and nearly dies.

Chapter 7

After his accident, Huw is bedridden for five years. His mother is also incapacitated for a while. She was pregnant and has gone into labor as a result of her fall. She gives birth to a daughter named Olwen, and Huw's sister-in-law Bronwen also gives birth to a boy named Gareth. Bronwen recovers quickly and takes over running the household, much to the chagrin of Huw'smother. When Huw'smother finally recovers, the family has a big celebration, marred only by an argument between Huw's brother Owen and the father of a girl with whom Owen has fallen in love, Marged.

Chapter 8

Owen breaks off his relationship with Marged, and she marries his brother Gwilym. However, Marged secretly still loves Owen. A new pastor, Mr. Gruffydd, begins visiting Huw and argues with a fundamentalist member of his congregation, Mr. Elias, who is upset that the minister allows festivities for Christmas.

Chapter 9

Mr. Gruffydd takes Huw to the mountains for his first outing since his accident, pushing Huw to try to recover, explaining that it is a question more of the spirit than of the body. Huw does seem to improve, but he also notices the great expansion of the slag heap, and he learns that the slag is killing the daffodils and the fish.

Chapter 10

Huw gets in trouble upon his first reappearance

in chapel. He inadvertently remains behind after the service and hears the deacons denouncing a young woman for having an affair, which prompts him to confront and criticize them. His father is mortified by his young son's challenge to the authorities, but his mother supports him.

Chapter 11

Both his father and Mr. Gruffydd scold Huw for speaking out against the deacons, stating that it was brave but misguided. They tell Huw that he does not truly understand, and he should respect his elders.

Chapter 12

After his wife dies, Ianto returns home. His return is highly celebrated, but he argues with Mr. Gruffydd over the role of preachers, saying they do nothing for the socioeconomic needs of their congregations.

Chapter 13

Ianto becomes more sympathetic to preachers despite their nonrevolutionary ways. Huw spies on a woman in childbirth. His father and Bronwen later reprimand him.

Chapter 14

Mr. Elias steals the Morgans' turkeys. Mr.

Gruffydd denounces the spread of thieving, warning that it will lead to the appearance of police, jails, and magistrates. He adds that the real enemy is coal, as it symbolizes money and can instill greed in the townspeople.

Chapter 15

Huw's sister Angharad is secretly seeing a local mine owner's son, Iestyn Evans. When her brothers find out, they threaten to beat up Iestyn for not asking permission first. Another sister, Ceridwen, is getting properly engaged, as is Davy. However, Marged, who has never overcome her love for Owen even though she married Gwilym, commits suicide by throwing herself in a fire.

Chapter 16

Huw goes to the National School. He does well in his entrance exams, but he fights with his fellow students and is at odds with his teacher, Mr. Jonas-Sessions. At home his father teaches him how to fight.

Chapter 17

Chapter 17 marks a special episode of vigilante justice (taking the law into one's own hands) in which the village men, led by the minister, go searching in the slums among foreigners and people of mixed blood for the rapist and murderer of a young girl. When they find him, they hand him over to the girl's family, who burns him to death. Meanwhile, Huw takes boxing lessons from trained boxers, Dai Bando and Cyfartha Lewis.

Chapter 18

Huw fights in school again and is caned by the teacher. He goes up on the mountain and has a vision of the valley being depleted of its riches.

Chapter 19

The students who mocked Huw when he first attended school are now in awe of his fighting prowess. Ceinwen Phillips, the sister of a boy he fought and beat, seems interested in him, but he is more interested in Shani Hughes. Huw's boxer friends beat up the teacher who caned him.

Chapter 20

Another strike occurs and lasts for months. Huw's father is ashamed, because the men's actions mean the women and children will go hungry. Shops close, and children die. After many months of striking, the men return to work, gaining one concession concerning a minimum wage for their work.

Chapter 21

When his teacher grabs him by the ear, Huw hits him. He has to speak to the headmaster as a result, but the headmaster is sympathetic and finds a new teacher for Huw and reassigns his old teacher to the lowest grade level. However, Mr. Gruffydd reprimands Huw for hitting an authority figure. Meanwhile, Angharad must choose between two suitors: Iestyn Evans, the rich son of the recently deceased local mine owner, and Mr. Gruffydd, the poor preacher.

Chapter 22

Huw's sister Ceridwen is getting married, and Huw gets his first suit with long trousers from the tailors, who joke in front of him in a way he does not understand; he is frustrated that no one will explain the jokes to him. Huw helps Mr. Gruffydd with carpentry.

Chapter 23

Huw's sister Angharad agrees to marry the rich dandy Iestyn, even though they squabble constantly and she really loves Mr. Gruffydd. But Mr. Gruffydd tells her he is too poor to support her and too old to be her husband.

Huw seeks answers to questions about sex and finally has them explained in a way by Mr. Gruffydd, in religious terms. Earlier he kissed his sister-in-law Bronwen in a nonbrotherly way.

Chapter 24

Huw feels like a man now that he has a suit and has developed physically, but he fears his new situation and almost wishes he was a boy again. The family gathers for the weddings of Davy and Ceridwen; at the events, there is a choir, a harpist, and even a rugby match. Ceinwen Phillips pursues Huw, who at first puts her off.

Chapter 25

The choir, led by Huw's brother Ivor, is invited to perform for the Queen.

Chapter 26

Ceinwen Phillips convinces Huw to go up the mountain to listen to nightingales. They stay for a very long time, and her family comes looking for her. Huw has to sneak off. The family continues searching, threatening a war if they find out who was with her.

Chapter 27

Ivor's choir returns from performing for the Queen at Windsor Castle. They have a large celebration; Huw's father and mother are very proud of Ivor.

Huw is eligible for a scholarship to university, but just before finishing his exams, he sees a Welsh girl being punished for speaking Welsh by his old teacher, Mr. Jonas-Sessions. Infuriated, Huw attacks the teacher and nearly kills him. He escapes arrest but is expelled from school. His father says that he told Huw to fight.

Huw goes to apologize to his teacher, but the teacher insults him and Huw withdraws his apology. Huw can still apply to university but now decides he wants to be a coal miner like the rest of his family.

Chapter 28

Mr. Gruffydd looks old and worn. Huw wants to offer him support but is not sure how to do so. Mr. Gruffydd remarks that he has grown old without achieving anything.

Chapter 29

In chapter 29, Huw goes to work in the mines and describes what it is like inside them. He recounts the terror, the dark, the screaming wind, and the sheer joy of returning to the surface. Word comes that Angharad's husband is headed to South Africa to arrange coal for the Navy in the new war there (presumably the Boer War of 1899-1902).

Chapter 30

Huw goes up on the mountain again with Ceinwen, and the two have a romantic encounter. He later takes her to the theater, but the theater comes under attack from religious extremists who call acting sinful. Huw, along with his boxing friends, fights the extremists.

Owen marries Blodwen, the sister of Iestyn Evans, in London, and he and Gwilym go to America. The sudden marriage and departure upset their mother.

Chapter 31

Angharad returns for a visit, looking old, tired, and gray. Bronwen has a baby boy named Taliesin, and the family experiences much happiness. However, a month later, Ivor (Bronwen's husband and Huw's brother) dies in a cave-in.

Chapter 32

Huw's mother is angry over the loss of her son. She also thinks Bronwen will need a new husband, but this idea inspires jealousy in Huw, who loves Bronwen himself, though he says not in a romantic way. He does go to live with her for a while, just as a companion, but they live awkwardly together.

Chapter 33

While Davy helps plan a new strike, Ianto leaves the coal mines for the ironworks. Huw also plans to leave the mines for ironworking but talks of his preference for woodworking. Angharad incites gossip by spending time with Mr. Gruffydd while her husband is away in South Africa, and Huw and

Bronwen try to deal with their difficult and ambiguous relationship.

Chapter 34

Back in the mines, Huw gets into yet another fight, this time over slighting remarks made about his sister Angharad. Fired from his job, he decides to take up carpentry.

Chapter 35

Huw is forced to go to court over his latest fight, but the charges are dismissed when the victim refuses to press them, wanting no part of court justice. At home, Huw finds out that the deacons have voted to dismiss Mr. Gruffydd, who will apparently go to Patagonia in South America.

Chapter 36

With Mr. Gruffydd departing, the chapel congregation splits in two.

Chapter 37

Huw's boxing friends take part in a prizefight for money. Huw joins them reluctantly. Despite his frequent fighting, he thinks fighting for money is wrong, especially in front of spectators, whom he calls cattle.

Huw's friend Dai wins the prizefight, but he

nearly goes blind in the process. Nonetheless, Dai and Cyfartha take home enough money to buy a pub.

Chapter 38

Huw becomes a master carpenter. Looking back, he thinks he was happy sharing a house with Bronwen and her children, but at the time their odd relationship continues to cause awkwardness between them. Also, gossip prompts Huw to want to fight yet again, but Bronwen restrains him.

Chapter 39

The slag continues to bother Huw, but others, including his father, seem resigned to its expansion. Davy has to fight a court case and then decides to immigrate to New Zealand. Ianto plans to leave for Germany. Hardly anyone is left, their father observes.

Chapter 40

Another strike begins after much talk of Socialism among the union men. Huw thinks that they are turning to foreign principles, and when one of the strikers makes a slighting remark to his sister because of the family's connection to mine owners, he nearly starts another fight.

Earlier, though, he had an enjoyable experience taking Bronwen shopping. After the union meeting he has a vision of marching, singing men, lifting his spirits with a prayer.

Chapter 41

Huw and the boxers are unhappy about the strike but are also upset that Winston Churchill, the Home Secretary, has sent English soldiers to deal with the situation. A riot breaks out; a mob smashes shop windows and threatens to flood the pits. Huw and the boxers make sure the pumps keep working, helping the management.

Chapter 42

In the final chapter, the strike brings yet another tragedy to the Morgan family. Huw's father dies in a cave-in when he investigates a possible flooding in the mine, which the strikers' actions may have caused.

Huw closes the narrative by lamenting that in the thirty years since his father's death, he has failed to leave his mark on the world. Now, almost everyone in his story is gone, though not entirely gone, because they linger in his memory. He reasons that if they are truly dead, then everyone is dead. He resists making such a conclusion, though he ends his story by looking backward at his green valley, as if to say that it is gone too.

Characters

Idris Atkinson

Idris Atkinson, who lives in the poorest section of the village among the Irish and English immigrants and the mixed-blood Welsh, is found guilty of attacking a young girl by a vigilante mob and handed over to the girl's family for execution.

Dai Bando

Dai Bando is one of the boxers who teaches Huw how to fight. He nearly loses his eyesight in a prizefight.

Mr. Abishai Elias

Mr. Abishai Elias, a shopkeeper and a deacon at the chapel, thinks the pastor Mr. Gruffydd is not strict enough and becomes an enemy of the Morgan family.

Blodwen Evans

Blodwen Evans, the sister of Iestyn Evans, becomes interested in Owen Morgan and eventually marries him.

Iestyn Evans

Iestyn Evans, the son of a local mine owner, is a rich dandy who pursues and eventually marries Angharad Morgan. He and Angharad fight constantly during their engagement and are referred to as Kiss and Scratch. He goes off to South Africa during the war there (presumably the Boer War of 1899-1902).

Old Mr. Evans

Old Mr. Evans, Iestyn Evans's father, is a local mine owner who treats his men better than the large mine owners do. He dies in a mine accident.

Mr. Gruffydd

Mr. Gruffydd is the new pastor at the Morgans' chapel when Huw is bedridden. He helps Huw with his recovery, and in general, he serves as Huw's mentor. He is portrayed as sympathetic to the miners' cause, though he also believes in moderation. Mr. Gruffydd and Huw's sister Angharad Morgan fall in love, but he sends her away from him, thinking she should not marry a poor and old man like himself. However, when Angharad is unhappy in her marriage to Iestyn Evans, Mr. Gruffydd spends time with her, inciting gossip and leading the chapel deacons to dismiss him. He leaves Huw's village, apparently for Patagonia in South America.

Shani Hughes

Shani Hughes, a girl at school whom Huw likes, moves away before he gets to know her well.

Mrs. Tom Jenkins

Mrs. Tom Jenkins, the wife of an incapacitated miner, is Huw's first teacher. She is bitter over her husband's fate.

Mr. Elijah Jonas-Sessions

Mr. Elijah Jonas-Sessions, or Mr. Jonas for short, is Huw's teacher at the National School. He takes an instant dislike to Huw, apparently because Huw is from a Welsh-speaking coal mining family and Mr. Jonas looks down on the coal miners and tries to seem English rather than Welsh. When Huw witnesses Mr. Jonas-Sessions punishing a Welsh girl for speaking Welsh, he becomes infuriated and attacks the teacher, nearly killing him.

Media Adaptations

- *How Green Was My Valley* was adapted to film and directed by John Ford in 1941. Starring Walter Pidgeon, Maureen O'Hara, and Roddy McDowall, the film won five Academy Awards including for best picture in 1942. It was produced by Twentieth Century-Fox.

- *How Green Was My Valley*, an eight-part miniseries in black and white, was produced by the British Broadcasting Corporation Television (BBC TV) in 1960. It was directed and produced by Dafydd Gruffydd and starred Eynon Evans and Rachel Thomas.

- *How Green Was My Valley* (1975-76), a six-part Masterpiece Theatre presentation, was coproduced by Twentieth Century-Fox Television and BBC TV. It was directed by Ronald Wilson and starred Stanley Baker and John Clive.

- *A Time for Singing*, a musical adaptation of the novel, was produced on Broadway for forty-one performances in 1966. The performance included music, lyrics, and a book by Gerald Freedman and

John Morris.

- *How Green Was My Valley* was issued as an unabridged audiobook by Chivers Audio Books in 1992.

Cyfartha Lewis

Cyfartha Lewis is one of the boxers who teaches Huw how to fight.

Meillyn Lewis

Meillyn Lewis is a young woman punished by the deacons for having an affair.

Angharad Morgan

Angharad Morgan, one of Huw's sisters, is lively in her youth but becomes old and tired after making a "suitable" marriage to the heir of a mine owner instead of marrying the man she truly loves, Mr. Gruffydd.

Beth Morgan

Beth Morgan, the mother of the Morgan family, is a traditional homemaker, though she acts nontraditionally in making a threatening speech to the miners' union. She is incapacitated for a significant portion of the novel after she falls in the snow and Huw rescues her but almost dies himself.

Like her husband, Beth loses control of her household, giving way to her daughter-in-law Bronwen. She also loses some of Huw's respect when he sees her crying weakly.

Bronwen Morgan

Bronwen enters the story early on as the wife of Huw's eldest brother, Ivor. As a child, Huw feels that he is in love with Bronwen. Bronwen takes over running the Morgan household when Huw's mother is unable to due to her accident, and she functions as a sort of surrogate mother to Huw. After Ivor's death, Huw moves in with Bronwen and her two children in a platonic but ambiguous relationship.

Ceridwen Morgan

Ceridwen Morgan, Huw's sister, marries in a double ceremony at the same time as her brother Davy.

Davy Morgan

Davy Morgan is the most militant of the Morgan sons. He is involved in organizing a union and gives speeches to the men. He moves out of the Morgan house after having a falling out with his father over union matters and marries in a double ceremony at the same time as his sister Ceridwen.

Gwilym Morgan

Another of Huw's brothers, the younger Gwilym marries Marged after Owen rejects her. He and Owen later leave Wales, first for London, England, and then for the United States.

Mr. Gwilym Morgan

The father of the Morgan family is a coal miner and the informal leader of his fellow coal miners in the early stages of the novel, but his leadership is challenged in the course of the story by more radical men in the developing miners' union. Some of these radicals are his own sons, especially Davy, and he loses control not only within the community as a whole but within his own household. As others become more radical, he becomes closer to management, accepting a promotion to superintendent. In the end, he tries to protect the mines from the effects of the strike, an action that costs him his life.

Huw Morgan

Huw Morgan, the narrator of the novel, is also its central figure. In some respects, *How Green Was My Valley* is a family saga and the tale of a whole community. Yet at heart it is Huw's story, the story of a young boy growing up and finding his way in life. The time frame of the narrative is left deliberately vague in the book, but Huw's father mentions that young Huw is six years old in an early chapter; his growth through adolescence to young adulthood is traced in subsequent chapters. As narrator, Huw seems to be in his early sixties, writing long after the events discussed have passed.

Huw presents himself as endearingly innocent, though he is clearly a feisty, fiery-tempered boy and young adult, ready to fight at the slightest provocation. He also becomes the family's intellectual, perhaps in part because of his several years as an invalid, during which he spends much of his time reading. In a family of coal miners, Huw is the only one who goes to secondary school and studies for examinations that will get him into college. Characteristically, his temper, along with his stubbornness, keeps him from that goal. He ultimately renounces the life of the mind, much to his father's dismay. He decides instead to follow the family trade of coal mining and, when that trade does not work out, he becomes a carpenter.

Huw rhapsodizes about carpentry and makes profound-sounding statements throughout the novel. He also speaks enthusiastically about women and love, and the novel follows him through his romantic awakening with Ceinwen Phillips and his ambiguous love for his sister-in-law Bronwen.

As the elderly narrator, Huw presents himself as a disappointed and nostalgic man, stating that he has failed to make his mark in life and expressing sadness over the disappearance of his friends and family and his valley.

Ianto Morgan

Huw's second-oldest brother, Ianto, leaves the family early in the story when he marries a woman of whom they do not fully approve, but he returns after she dies and becomes caught up in the union struggles. He later immigrates to Germany.

Ivor Morgan

Huw's oldest brother, Ivor, marries Bronwen early in the novel. He is close to his father, taking his side against the union radicals, and he leads the village choir. His major triumph is taking the choir to sing for Queen Victoria. Halfway through the story, Ivor dies in a mining accident, leaving Bronwen a widow.

Marged Morgan

Marged falls in love with Owen Morgan, but when he rejects her in the wake of her father's complaints about their relationship, she marries Owen's brother Gwilym. She never gets over Owen, however, and eventually goes mad and commits suicide by jumping into a fire.

Olwen Morgan

Olwen, Huw's youngest sister, is born after their mother's fall on the mountain. When Huw leaves the village, Olwen seems to be the only one left to say good-bye to.

Owen Morgan

Owen, another of Huw's brothers, is interested in mechanical inventions and moves first to London and then to America to pursue a business career. Early in the book, he has a relationship with a girl named Marged, but leaves her after her father makes a public complaint about them, devastating her. Much later in the story, Owen marries Blodwen Evans.

Mr. Motshill

Mr. Motshill, the headmaster at the National School, is sympathetic to Huw.

Ceinwen Phillips

Ceinwen Phillips is the sister of a boy Huw beats in a fight at school. She becomes interested in Huw and they become involved romantically, but they drift apart.

Old Twm

Old Twm is assistant to Hwfa Williams, the tailor, with whom he is always arguing.

Hwfa Williams

Hwfa Williams, the tailor, fits Huw for his first adult suit.

Themes

Nostalgia

How Green Was My Valley is an evocation of a past that no longer exists, a time period that Huw praises as being far superior to his present time. His valley used to be green, as the title of the book states, but now it has become ravaged by a slag heap. Something has gone wrong with the world, he says; there used to be prosperity and happiness, but that has vanished. His own life has vanished, he states, without his having left a mark on the world, and all the people he knew have vanished as well. Huw's tone throughout the novel is a sad one as he remembers times gone by.

Ecology

Ahead of its time, the book deals with the destruction of the environment, showing how the green valley has become black with slag, as human greed for nature's riches has led to the destruction of flowers on the mountain and fish in the river. Huw wonders how this could have been allowed to happen, but no one else seems even to notice or justify it by asking where else the slag could be put in order to preserve the environment.

Coming of Age

How Green Was My Valley details Huw's maturity into adulthood. He develops from an innocent child into a hot-tempered adolescent who eventually learns some of the mysteries of love. Huw must also decide on a career path. Although seemingly qualified for an intellectual future, Huw is drawn to his family's life of coal mining.

Unions, Socialism, and Revolution

Much of *How Green Was My Valley* focuses on the struggles of the coal miners, some of whom are drawn to union organizing and Socialism. The book explores pro-and antiunion positions and moderation versus extremism. Some of the characters refer to the German Socialist philosopher Karl Marx and the British Socialists Keir Hardie and Henry Hyndman. However, actual analysis of Socialist ideology rarely occurs, and the thrust of the book refutes such thinking. Strikes occur several times in the novel, and at first it seems that the workers are justified. In the climactic strike, however, the workers appear selfish and greedy, and the main effect of strikes is human suffering: children starve and shops shut down.

Welshness

In many ways, the book is a celebration of Welsh traditions, including choral singing, rugby, and Nonconformist religion. It also honors the Welsh language and the fight to preserve the language from English. The very syntax (sentence structure) of the book is part of this effort, as are the episodes at the National School in which Huw struggles against restrictions on the Welsh language. The book at times seems ethnocentric (characterized by a belief that one's own group is superior to another) in suggesting that immigrants to Wales, notably the Irish and English in the poor section of the village, have a bad effect on the community. Similarly, Mr. Morgan's rejection of Marx and other Socialists is cast in terms of their foreign status. He states that Wales is for the Welsh.

Gender Roles and Parental Control

How Green Was My Valley depicts a traditional domestic society under threat. The two maternal women in the novel, Huw's mother and Bronwen, focus almost entirely on domestic matters involved with running the household and do not work outside the home. Huw's father is the patriarch of the family and holds ultimate authority—at least until his sons revolt against his moderate politics. Afterwards, he declares that he is no longer in charge of the family, and they are all equal lodgers in the household he once ruled. Huw's mother also revolts, first by speaking at a union meeting and later by complaining that she was never taught the arithmetic that young Huw is learning. Later in the novel, Bronwen revolts against Huw's notions of male-female relations. She tells him she is not his brother's possession, and it is her decision who shares her world. Huw, however, remains caught up in romantic notions about women and the world they bring to men.

Topics for Further Study

- Research the history of Welsh nationalism. Write a paper explaining how Wales came to be controlled by England and how the Welsh have resisted or accepted English rule over the years.

- Explore the history of religious Nonconformity in Britain. What did it mean to be a Nonconformist? How were the Nonconformists connected to the Puritans of earlier ages? Give an oral presentation explaining these points and also explaining what religious groups in the United States are similar to the Nonconformists.

- Imagine what it would be like to

spend several months or years bedridden. Write a short story or poem about the possible experience, including how you would occupy your time and communicate with others.

- Produce a video about Wales today and how it differs from the Wales presented in *How Green Was My Valley*. Try to incorporate the music of Welsh singers in the film.

- Organize a class debate over whether unions are positive or negative organizations. The debate might focus on the effect of strikes on the strikers, the owners, and the public. It might also include discussions of how unions are organized and regulated, and how they interact with other members of society.

- Prepare a multimedia presentation on coal mining. How was it done in the past? How is it done now? What are the effects of coal mining on human health and the environment?

Romantic Misalliances

The novel abounds with frustrated

relationships. Angharad is in love with Mr. Gruffydd, but she marries Iestyn Evans, sentencing herself to an unhappy marriage which ages her before her time. Mr. Gruffydd, who returns Angharad's feelings, loses much of his spirit after her marriage to Iestyn. After Owen rejects Marged, she marries his brother Gwilym. She never gets over Owen, and eventually goes mad and commits suicide by jumping into a fire. Huw never marries, living in the memory of his early girlfriend, Ceinwen, and in frustrated longing for his sister-in-law, Bronwen, who suffers the loss of her husband in a mine accident. Ianto also loses his wife. Derrick Price, in his article in *The Progress of Romance*, suggests that these problems reflect the breakdown of traditional life under the pressure of new forces.

Style

Symbolism

Symbolism is a literary device in which an object is used to represent an idea or concept. The chief symbol in the novel is the slag heap, the pile of refuse left over from coal mining. The slag heap accumulates in the valley and up the mountainside to such an extent that by the time Huw leaves the village, it is set to destroy the house in which he lives as well as other homes. Described as almost glacier-like, the slag is a slowly advancing inexorable force. Huw says the house is well built, but even it will be flattened by the advancing slag. The works of human beings are no match for the forces of nature, especially a nature that has been ravaged by human beings in the pursuit of the profits of coal mining. The slag heap can be interpreted as nature's revenge and a symbol of the defeat of human beings.

The coal pits may also be symbolic. The word "pit" is used elsewhere in the novel to mean hell, which suggests that going down into the pits is like descending into hell. When Huw finally enters the pits, he is terrified by the absolute darkness and screeching wind. Conversely, at the beginning of the novel, working in the coal pits appears to be a noble occupation.

Fire is a dual symbol in the novel. The fire

consumes and kills Marged as she commits suicide, representing suffering, madness, and death. However, fire warms Huw and Ceinwen when they are on the mountain, representing comfort and security. Fire can be interpreted as either a positive or negative symbol in the book.

Syntax and Tone

Though writing in English, Llewellyn uses exotic syntax (sentence structure) to convey a sense of Welshness. The characters are all supposed to be speaking in Welsh, and Llewellyn tries to convey this fact by various constructions, notably starting a sentence or phrase with "There is." For instance: "There is clever you are," "there is heavy my mother seemed to me," and "there is pleased she was." He also uses inversion (reversing sentence components) for the same effect: "Saying nothing against Ivor I was."

Llewellyn's tone is also somewhat biblical or mystical. Huw often utters statements that appear profound, even if the subject matter is seemingly insignificant. The content is not actually philosophical, but the air of profundity, the reverential tone, creates a magical aura around the language, such that even if readers do not feel they have been transported to exotic Wales, they may at least experience a realm of fantasy or mystery.

Flashbacks and Foreshadowing

How Green Was My Valley is framed as a flashback from Huw's present to his early life, and this structure seems a completely natural complement to the book's theme of nostalgia. Huw also occasionally lets the reader know that something is coming before he presents it, thus foreshadowing to create interest and suspense. For instance, before presenting his denunciation of the deacons at chapel, Huw announces that on his first return to services he disgraced himself forever but was not sorry.

South Wales Coalfield

Coal mining transformed the southeast part of Wales in the second half of the nineteenth century, particularly in the valleys of the Rhondda District in Glamorgan County. The population in the Rhondda increased from one thousand or two thousand in 1851 to 113,000 in 1901. As in the novel, a string of connected villages sprang up in the valleys, as there was not room for large towns or cities, and the amount of coal exported rose from 450,000 tons to almost thirty-seven million tons. Also, large slag heaps were created which moved and threatened towns. As late as 1966, the waste from a coal slag tip buried part of the village of Aberfan, killing more than one hundred children.

Unions and Socialism

The book's depiction of the growth of unionism reflects the actual events of the time period from the 1870s until 1910. With the growth of the coal industry, coal miners attempted to organize and affiliate with unions elsewhere. Early attempts to unionize in the 1870s failed, and the mine owners were able to impose the sliding scale system referred to in the novel, under which miners' pay fluctuated according to the price of coal. In 1898 a long strike and lockout over the sliding scale took place, much like the lengthy strike in chapter 20 of the novel. As in the novel, the strike produced much suffering and radicalized the miners, so that they turned away from moderate leaders (like Huw's father in the novel) and created the more radical South Wales Miners' Federation.

Compare & Contrast

- **1900:** Coal mining is at its peak in Wales, and slag heaps begin to take over the valleys.

  1939: After two decades of economic slump and depression, the Welsh coal mining industry is in crisis.

  Today: Coal mining has almost disappeared from Wales, and the valleys have been cleaned up and made green again as tourist locations.

- **1900:** Welsh seems to be a language in decline; many Welsh people prefer to speak English.

  1939: Efforts begin to revive the Welsh language.

  Today: Welsh can be heard in Wales on radio and television and can be seen on bilingual road signs, but English is the everyday language for most Welsh people.

- **1900:** Welsh choirs become world renowned, and Wales is known as a land of song.

  1939: With the advent of the gramophone, radio, and other leisure pursuits, Welsh choirs go into decline.

  Today: Modern Welsh people pursue a variety of leisure activities, and Welsh choirs are mostly a thing of the past.

- **1900:** Wales is ruled by England and has no independent government or local autonomy. However, a politician of Welsh descent, David Lloyd George, rises to become Prime Minister of England.

  1939: A Welsh nationalist party, Plaid Cymru, has been formed but wins little support for Welsh independence or autonomy.

  Today: The Welsh have their own National Assembly and have some autonomy within the United Kingdom.

In 1910 a strike against the Cambrian Combine mining company led to riots in the town of

Tonypandy, prompting Winston Churchill, the Home Secretary, to send first police and then soldiers, events depicted and referred to at the end of the novel. Within two years, radicals issued a Socialist tract, *The Miners' Next Step*, but despite talk of Marxism and Socialism, the Welsh miners ended the strike by becoming supporters of the newly formed and relatively moderate Labour Party rather than starting a revolution.

Nonconformist Religion

The novel uses the word *chapel* rather than *church* to refer to houses of worship, reflecting the fact that the majority of the Welsh belonged to Nonconformist religious denominations. The established Church of England (the Anglicans) had churches but was a minority religion in Wales. The Nonconformists, including Baptists, Methodists, and other Protestants outside the Church of England, attended chapel. Nonconformists dominated Wales in the late nineteenth century. As a very religious, puritanical society, Wales had a chapel for every four hundred people in 1914.

Choral Singing

Simultaneous with the rise of Nonconformity and the coal industry in the late nineteenth century, the Welsh became noted for their choral singing. Most choral singing was associated with chapels, though it sometimes took place at cultural festivals known as *eisteddfodau*. Both mixed and male choirs were popular. The Treorchy Male Choir, composed primarily of coal miners, was invited to Windsor Castle to perform for Queen Victoria in 1895, much as Ivor's choir does in the novel.

Welsh Language and Nationalism

At the end of the nineteenth century, Wales was in the unusual position of having a national language (Welsh) that no more than half the population spoke. Wales had lost its independence to England centuries before, eventually becoming part of the United Kingdom. In *How Green Was My Valley*, Llewellyn implies that Welsh was suppressed by the English, who forced Welsh children to speak English at school. However, active suppression of Welsh in Wales may be less important than the influx of English immigrants, the proximity of Wales to England, and the collective belief in English as the language of the future.

In fact, attempts to revive Welsh began as early as the 1890s and continued into the twentieth century. The Welsh nationalist party, Plaid Cymru, rose during the twentieth century, ultimately winning local autonomy and a National Assembly for Wales at the end of the century.

Depression and War

Llewellyn published *How Green Was My Valley* long after the events depicted in it occurred, following two decades of economic difficulties in

Wales resulting from the decline of the coalfield and one decade of a worldwide depression. Moreover, the book was published just a month after the outbreak of World War II in Europe, a time period of great difficulties.

Critical Overview

Writing in 1983 in the *Dictionary of Literary Biography*, Mick Felton comments that because Llewellyn was not part of mainstream modern literature, he received little academic attention. With the appearance of some major academic studies of Welsh writing in English after 2000, the situation changed somewhat, but the academics who do write about Llewellyn tend to be critical of his work. The original reviewers of *How Green Was My Valley*, at least those outside Wales, praised the book highly. Richard Church, as reported by John Harris in his article in *Welsh Writing in English*, saw in it "the freshness of folk song and the old Celtic tales." In Wales, though the book was as popular with the public as it was elsewhere, reviewers called it "trash," according to David Smith (also known as Dai Smith) in his article in the *Anglo-Welsh Review*. Later Welsh academic critics have condemned the book for perpetuating stereotypes. Some have been more positive in their reviews than others. Although Glyn Jones calls the novel "literary hokum" in his book *The Dragon Has Two Tongues: Essays on Anglo-Welsh Writers and Writing* and in private correspondence called it a fake, he admits that he found it absorbing to read. He praises its interesting characters, humor, and drama while also noting its use of clichés.

Smith, though conceding the novel's appeal, condemns it as "a gargantuan con-trick" similar to a "tawdry Hollywood 'B' picture," a description he removed in a later reprinting of his article. Stephen Knight criticizes the book even more. In his book *A Hundred Years of Fiction: Writing Wales in English* he sees even its popularity as a sign of the forces at work against authenticity, adding that Llewellyn's novel is "a classic example of colonized writing … making the Welsh seem quaint but willing servants of English capitalism." In an essay in *Welsh Writing in English*, Knight contrasts *How Green Was My Valley* with the more documentary, realist, and radical writings of other authors of the 1930s, criticizing Llewellyn's book for being too personalized and sentimental, in effect failing to be a Socialist novel.

Even so, *How Green Was My Valley* has some academic defenders. Whereas other academics have criticized Llewellyn for inaccuracy, Harris reports on Llewellyn's account of his research for the book, which he discarded in order to get closer to the characters in his story. For Harris, this is a candid explanation of how fiction writers work; they write imaginative stories, not documentaries. Harris goes on to praise *How Green Was My Valley* for its mythic, romantic evocation of a past golden age, the very quality that other academics condemn. Harris says that Llewellyn "taps into the elemental."

Derrick Price, in an essay in *The Progress of Romance: The Politics of Popular Fiction*, also distances himself from those who condemn *How Green Was My Valley* for inaccuracies, conservative politics, and sentimentality. Though he acknowledges the validity of some of those criticisms, he also describes the novel as "an interesting, complex, and even a key text in the body of writing about the industrial valleys of South Wales." At the same time, Price distinguishes *How Green Was My Valley* from another genre of the time period, the documentary novel; in Llewellyn's book, specific dates and place names are deliberately missing. Price states, "Instead, we are taken to a mythic past" by "an almost perfect narrator." In one of the few full-length academic articles written about the novel, Price provides a detailed examination of Huw as narrator and analyzes other aspects of the novel, including its depiction of gender relations, the symbol of the slag heap, and the pressure of new forces on old traditions. He concludes by saying that the power of the book "derives from the way in which it uses romance to take real historical struggles and return them to us as an ineluctable fall from grace of particular human beings."

In short, several reviewers have criticized *How Green Was My Valley* as a failed documentary novel, but others have praised it as a successful attempt to create something quite different from documentary realism—a timeless, universal story about the disappearance of a past golden age.

What Do I Read Next?

- *None But the Lonely Heart* (1943) was Llewellyn's next novel after *How Green Was My Valley*. It differs from the latter, as a tale of criminal life in London.

- *Coal: A Human History* (2003), by Barbara Freese is a popular survey of the mining and use of coal dating back to the Middle Ages and covering not just England and Wales but also the United States and China.

- *Caverns of Night: Coal Mines in Art, Literature, and Film* (2000), edited by William B. Thesing, is a collection of essays analyzing books and films about coal mining.

- *Sons and Lovers* (1913), by D. H. Lawrence, is a groundbreaking work of fiction set in an English coal mining district.

- For a Socialist novel about American coal mining, see Upton Sinclair's *King Coal* (1917).

- *Power* (1962), by Howard Fast, is a later novel about coal mining and unions in America.

- For another Welsh novel about coal mining, see *The Red Hills* (1932), by Rhys Davies.

- *Rasselas* (1759), by Samuel Johnson, is a classic tale of a young boy who has to leave a "happy valley" to discover the meaning of life.

- Joseph Conrad's tale of Africa, *Heart of Darkness* (1902), is another story about failed heroism with mythic overtones.

- For a nostalgic poem about nature and loss, see "Ode: Intimations of Immortality" by William Wordsworth, first published in *Poems, in Two Volumes* (1807).

Sources

Davies, John, *A History of Wales*, rev. ed., Penguin Books, 2007, pp. 310-711.

Felton, Mick, "Richard Llewellyn," in *Dictionary of Literary Biography*, Vol. 15, *British Novelists, 1930-1959*, edited by Bernard Oldsey, Gale Research, 1983, p. 323.

Harris, John, "Popular Images," in *A Guide to Welsh Literature*, Vol. 7, *Welsh Writing in English*, edited by M. Wynn Thomas, University of Wales Press, 2003, pp. 207-208, 210.

Hopkins, Chris, "Depressed Pastorals? Documenting Wales in the 1930s," in *English Fiction in the 1930s: Language, Genre, History*, Continuum International Publishing Group, 2006, p. 74.

Jenkins, Geraint H., *A Concise History of Wales*, Cambridge University Press, 1984, pp. 173-306.

Jones, Glyn, *The Dragon Has Two Tongues: Essays on Anglo-Welsh Writers and Writing*, rev. ed., edited by Tony Brown, University of Wales Press, 2001, pp. 51, 53, 202.

Knight, Stephen, "'A New Enormous Music': Industrial Fiction in Wales," *A Guide to Welsh Literature*, Vol. 7, *Welsh Writing in English*, edited by M. Wynn Thomas, University of Wales Press, 2003, pp. 72-73.

———, "The Return of Romance: Richard Llewellyn," in *A Hundred Years of Fiction: Writing Wales in English*, University of Wales Press, 2004, p. 116.

Llewellyn, Richard, *How Green Was My Valley*, new ed., Michael Joseph, 1949.

Price, Derrick, "*How Green Was My Valley*: A Romance of Wales," in *The Progress of Romance: The Politics of Popular Fiction*, edited by Jean Radford, Routledge & Kegan Paul, 1986, pp. 73, 75, 79, 82-83, 93.

Smith, David, "Myth and Meaning in the Literature of the South Wales Coalfield—The 1930s," in the *Anglo-Welsh Review*, Vol. 25, No. 56, Spring 1976, pp. 29, 40.

Stephens, Meic, "Lloyd, Richard Dafydd Vivian Llewellyn," in *Oxford Dictionary of National Biography*, edited by H. C. G. Matthew and Brian Harrison, Vol. 34, Oxford University Press, 2004.

Williams, Gareth, *Valleys of Song: Music and Society in Wales, 1840-1914*, University of Wales Press, 1998.

Further Reading

Campbell, Joseph, *The Hero with a Thousand Faces*, Princeton University Press, 1968.

> This is Campbell's classic text on the myth of the hero, drawing on examples from classical mythology.

Edwards, Wil Jon, *From the Valley I Came*, Angus & Robertson, 1956.

> This is an autobiographical account by an actual miner of life in the mines and his involvement with Welsh nationalism and Socialism.

Herbert, Trevor, and Gareth Elwyn Jones, eds., *Wales, 1880-1914*, University of Wales Press, 1988.

> This collection includes historical essays on the period during which *How Green Was My Valley* is set.

Smith, Dai, *Wales: A Question for History*, Seren, 1999.

> Dai Smith (also known as David Smith), a Welsh historian and broadcaster, presents a number of essays on Welsh culture and history, including one that discusses *How Green Was My Valley*.

CPSIA information can be obtained
at www.ICGtesting.com
Printed in the USA
BVHW041835271118
534148BV00017B/312/P